Pebble® Plus

PIRATES AHOY!

Famous Pirates

by Rosalyn Tucker

Consulting editor: Gail Saunders-Smith, PhD

Raintree is an imprint of Capstone Global Library Limited, a company incorporated in England and Wales having its registered office at 7 Pilgrim Street, London, EC4V 6LB – Registered company number: 6695582

www.raintree.co.uk
myorders@raintree.co.uk

Text © Capstone Global Library Limited 2015
The moral rights of the proprietor have been asserted.

Editorial Credits
Michelle Hasselius, editor; Kazuko Collins, designer; Gina Kammer, media researcher; Gene Bentdahl, production specialist

ISBN 978 1 406 29350 0 (hardback)
19 18 17 16 15
10 9 8 7 6 5 4 3 2 1

ISBN 978 1 406 29355 5 (paperback)
20 19 18 17 16
10 9 8 7 6 5 4 3 2 1

British Library Cataloguing in Publication Data
A full catalogue record for this book is available from the British Library.

Photo Credits
Alamy: © Lebrecht Music and Arts Photo Library, 15, 19, © Steve Davey Photography, 17; AP Images: ASSOCIATED PRESS/ Brennan Linsley, 21; Bridgeman Images: © Look and Learn/Private Collection/Captain Kidd, Coton, Graham (1926–2003), 7, © Look and Learn/Private Collection/Captain Kidd, privateer or pirate? (gouache on paper), Petts, Kenneth John (1907–92), 5, © Look and Learn/Private Collection/Pirate, English School, (20th century), 13, Museum Purchase/Delaware Art Museum, Wilmington, USA/The Buccaneer Was a Picturesque Fellow, from 'The Fate of Treasure Town' by Howard Pyle, published in Harper's Monthly Magazine, December 1905 (oil on canvas), Pyle, Howard (1853–1911), cover, Peter Newark Historical Pictures/ Private Collection/Henry Avery (coloured engraving), English School, 9; Getty Images: Universal Images Group, 11; Shutterstock: newyear (ship silhouette), cover
Design elements: Shutterstock: A-R-T (old paper), La Gorda (rope illustration), vovan (old wood)

Printed in China.

Contents

The Golden Age

Daring pirates sailed the seas during

the Golden Age of Piracy (1690–1730).

They stole supplies and treasure

from towns and ships. Some pirates

became famous for their crimes.

William Kidd

Pirate William Kidd was paid to attack certain ships. Kidd kept the money. But he attacked any ships he chose.

William Kidd

Henry Every

Henry Every was a pirate

for only two years. In 1696

he raided a treasure ship.

Henry became the richest pirate

in the world in just one raid!

Henry Every

Stede Bonnet

Stede Bonnet was a rich landowner. He wanted to be a pirate. So he paid for his own ship. He even paid his crew with his own money.

Stede Bonnet

Blackbeard

Edward Teach was a feared

pirate known as Blackbeard.

He captured more than 40 ships.

Blackbeard got his name from

his thick, black beard.

Blackbeard

Black Bart

Bartholomew Roberts was Black Bart.

Black Bart was a famous pirate

from the Golden Age. He captured

more than 400 ships. Black Bart

died in battle in 1722.

Black Bart

Women pirates

Most pirates were men.

But a few women were also

famous pirates. Grace O'Malley

was a rich pirate from Ireland.

She owned at least five castles.

statue of
Grace O'Malley in
Westport, Ireland

Most pirate ships did not let
women on board. That did not
stop Anne Bonny and Mary Read.
They dressed up as men and
sailed with other pirates.

Anne Bonny and Mary Read

Pirates then and now

The Golden Age of Piracy is over.

But there are still pirates today.

They use small, fast boats

to attack ships. But just like all

pirates, they search for treasure.

modern pirates capture a ship

Glossary

attack try to hurt someone or something

capture take a person or place by force

crew team of people who work together

famous well known to many people

Golden Age of Piracy period from 1690 to 1730, when thousands of people became pirates around the world

landowner person who owns a large amount of land

pirate person who steals from ships and towns

raid sudden, surprise attack

supplies items needed to do a job or task

treasure gold, jewels, money or other items of value

Books

Pirates (It's Amazing!), Annabel Savery (Franklin Watts, 2013)

Pirates (Legends of the Sea), Rebecca Rissman (Raintree, 2011)

Top 10 Worst Nasty Pirates You Wouldn't Want to Meet, Fiona MacDonald (Book House, 2010)

Websites

www.bbc.co.uk/cbeebies/swashbuckle-online/games
Find the treasure and make the pirates walk the plank!
Try these fun pirate games.

www.jerseyheritage.org/learning/teacher-resources-pirates
Follow the links to discover the flags of Blackbeard and
Black Bart, and design your own Jolly Roger flag.

Index